STRING'S BOOK OF BENDERSKUM

From a different perspective

Rocky van de Benderskum

String

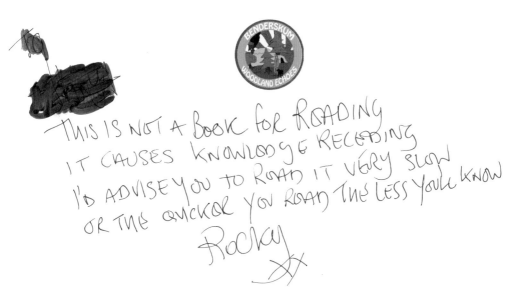

THIS IS NOT A BOOK FOR ROADING
IT CAUSES KNOWLODGE RECEDING
I'D ADVISE YOU TO ROAD IT VERY SLOW
OR THE QUICKOR YOU ROAD THE LESS YOU'LL KNOW
Rocky
xx

ISBN: 9798673622636

Cover design by: A benderskum
Library of String Number: 420 4 L1F3 (710)
Printed in (probably Poland) with ink on paper by clever people that can make computers do what they ask, rather than what the AI says

This book is dedicated to my dear friend Lou without whom I wouldn't be here today

Don't pass Audit Prg Uber Liebe René's Caine, Master, Master

A BENDERSKUM

CONTENTS

SIX WORD

Not the same as a foreword but it sounds a bit like two better at least in my head

As not everyone knows me, I felt an introduction wouldn't go amiss;

I'm String, the invisible friend of a benderskum, I've been around its entire life and due to the fibres of my soul and will probably, except in the event of an unfortunate fire, be around long after it's gone.

It has been suggested that I don't exist, except in the mind of a benderskum however if that were so, how could I be publishing a book.

If you are still unconvinced I'd like to direct you to pages where undeniable proof can be obtained.

First things first though I feel I need to warn any potential reader or even casual glancer the contents of this book will not improve your knowledge, it is in fact a book of unlearning the contents being designed to at least in a virtual way uneducate you.

You have been warned so the or fur and me accept no responsibilty for your plight

Below is an image of a benderskum, the tiny one with it's sibling and father, with me hiding in the background and the first time I was ever captured on film

BENDERSKUM
A CHIMERA

Ok so where did it begin the benderskum everyone I knew called me it, so the name change made sense and was legally done about 1995 but all the paperwork has been destroyed by a person I no longer associate with so I couldn't say for sure it was only my sur-name I changed.

I was born in 1958 with the name Rocky Paul Lau ☺ ☺ in Batu Gajah Malaysia, my old surname is however irrelevant as it isn't who I am anymore.

I first became a Cantheist in about 2003 when I still lived in the woods, which is the Cannabis religion, I am a part of is called Cantheism it is similar to pantheism but includes cannabis in the mix, explained more fully in 'What's in a benderskum' another book of utter drivel.

I first got into it because of research I was doing into the history of the plant giving birth to my belief that we as homo-sapiens co-evolved with cannabis, this belief is bolstered by the fact that we like every other vertebrate on the planet have an Endocan-nabinoid System; which was finally proven some 26 years or so ago, by some clever scientists.

As a boy I was in the merchant navy which is when I first tried cannabis at a night club in Quebec in 1974 it changed my life, I didn't last long in the navy as I was kicked out. I worked on a farm for a while then foolishly joined the army to shut my dad up, got stuck for four and a half years till I bought myself out. Rejoined the merchant navy became a chief petty officer but was sacked because the company hated unions and I was union rep. I drove a service bus in Dover for a couple of years, sold computers to shipping companies for a while. Then trained and worked as a tree surgeon and landscape gardener for about 5 years. I had my tools and vehicle stolen one night which put me out of business. Moved around a bit squatting all over the country ended up living in Pennypot Woods, Chartham, where I built with the help of the person I didn't mention before my first bender. Stayed there till the eviction that never was, the council paid people to move on, except me I told them to keep their money and moved to Blean Woods where I lived for way over a decade till 2003. I only moved back into society because I was very ill, had many tests to discover what was wrong but stopped all that when they suggested exploratory surgery, scary shit. I then had to just rest and recuperate.

Then in 2005 I stood for Parliament for the Legalise Cannabis Alliance. Did many speaking events and protests but it was all very exhausting.

In 2006 I got a job in Margate as a care worker for young deaf adults with other sometimes quite major disabilities and mental health conditions. I'd been able to sign since I was 13 when as I had undertaken voluntary work at a deaf club in St Margaret's Church, Canterbury which is these days the Canterbury Tales tourist attraction. I left in 2007 to work for Kent Autistic Trust in Gillingham to work with a deaf lad who had some hearing but wished to learn to speak, it took three months and he was able to communicate so didn't need my help any longer. Great but then I had no more work to do there, I was asked to transfer to another day care centre to work with three young deaf adults, they were great but my boss was inept and disliked me on sight, so mostly prevented me help them in achieving anything. I then recieved a call from someone at Westgate College for the deaf which was part of the Royal School for Deaf Children Margate to say they were recruiting and I would be welcome to come back. I went back as an educational support worker but in my spare time went to Christchurch University to study teaching. I then taught at the school and Westgate College in a project called the Orchard Shed Project which I also developed and managed and finally at Monkshill Farm which they also owned. I taught Horticulture for which I have 3 diplomas including the RHS General Certificate and Conservation Ecology for which I have no qualifications although I have studied the subject at University and attended many certificated courses. I also ran a small Forest School at the farm as I'm a qualified Forest School Leader. As a teacher my greatest joy was watching my students achieving things they always thought they couldn't. It was such a pleasure when a student visibly grasped a concept and could then impart that knowledge to their peers. Then in August 2013 I became very poorly my legs wouldn't carry me so teaching became problematic. The organisation I worked for decided to make me redundant which is of course illegal when a person is off sick, but I didn't have the energy to fight it. I had been diagnosed previous to this with osteoarthritis so I then had keyhole surgery on my left knee in the November after which they told me I have no cartilage whatsoever. Which explains why it's painful to walk as I walk bone on bone, it also wears out quickly so my knees are badly misshapen and walking is now even more painful added to which my knees just suddenly give way. They then told me within three months I would have a full knee replacement operation on my left knee. However on Valentine's day 2014 I was diagnosed with Acute Myeloid Leukaemia I was to be fair pretty poorly and it was most likely why I'd been poorly back in August. I was close to death, they did a bone marrow aspiration which involves drilling a hole into the hip bone and extracting bone marrow, which is to say the least a bit ouchy, as although they anaesthetised my hip it was only the flesh not the bone which really hurt both the drilling and during the aspiration. Instead of looking like blood it was grey green sludge. I asked one of the senior consultants what chance I have to survive this she said about 17% to which I replied ah no worries then double figures, fuck cancer. I then had months of chemotherapy in Kent and Canterbury Hospital, lost all my hair

3

and the use of my left arm well not all the use but it is quite numb after my radial nerve was damaged, wwhen inserting a (Peripherally Inserted Central Catheter) PICC line into my arm to administer the chemo stabbed into the nerve junction. At the end of July I was sent to Kings Hospital London for more chemo, pre-transplant teeth extractions and then my bone marrow transplant, which was the easy part, it was later in the day of the transplant when it got bad. The transplant itself was a hanging transfusion bag of stem cells, through a thing called a Hickman line which consisted of three tubes inserted in my chest through an incision pushed up under the skin over my collar bone then into a major vein that went straight into my heart, one tube being larger specifically for the transplant as it need to be completed in 25 minutes, I think any longer and it wouldn't work. About five hours later I started to hurt everywhere I was in the throes of Graft Versus Host Disease, which often happens after a transplant the immune system doesn't recognise the transplant so sends white blood cells, called T cells I think, to attack the invader. That's most transplants, bone marrow is different because it kind of is the immune system, as bone marrow makes your blood; both red and white corpuscles. So my immune system attacked all my organs, heart, lungs, brain, kidney, everything including the largest organ of all my skin, I was in agony, I have a very high pain threshold having fractured my skull in two places when I was 17, which gave me migraines my whole life until 2 years ago my friend Lou convinced me to go for a Daith piercing it's a bit inside the ear top at the front, she was was spot on not a single migraine since, some headaches but there's a universe of difference between the two. Anyway the GVHD settled down mostly with immunosuppressant meds, I still get it fairly regularly in my skin. The attack on my skin left it allergic to just about everything, soap, detergent, moisturisers, sun tan goop and very easy to break. It's all good though I'm a vegan vampire these days, which makes it of course problematic, for with social distancing it's difficult to bite a vegans neck from two metres. Let's see what else; I have osteopenia, hyperthyroidism and fungal pneumonia from all the chemo, radioactive stuff and genetically modified hormones they pumped into me. I have to carry a card in case of accident I if I need a blood transfusion it needs to be irradiated or it will clot. I have COPD no doubt from years of smoking tobacco, I also gave that up which was easy, I'd never tried before, I just decided I no longer smoked and I didn't no withdrawals, I'm strong minded and believe myself and not just in myself. The walking sticks I use well they remain in place they won't give me the knee operations because they don't think my body would hack it, ah well limp along I will then. Still fairly active in the anti cannabis prohibition movement which these days is becoming more like a farce written by Gilbert and Sullivan, with big businesses linked to members of the government growing tons of cannabis under licence. Apparently they legalised cannabis in 2018 for medicinal purposes whilst cannabis remains a schedule one substance meaning it has no medicinal value yet as I...oxymoronic springs to mind

One last thing the Chimera bit; in humans microchimerism is common in infants carrying the cells of their mother, these gradually disappear with age. In my case I am what is known as full donor chimera which means my DNA is different to the DNA I had 7 years ago. As my donor was a female my blood is genetically completely female which proved to be a bonus the two times I came out of remission the consultants, spotted male blood cells in one of my four times a week blood-letting sessions (that's what they felt like anyway), which they then adjusted the chemical stew they were giving me. The first time I wondered how they knew so I asked as usually it was by aspiration and as I said they were painful things and I hadn't had one, I would definitely have noticed. When they told me I had female blood I at first just laughed until I realised they were serious. Whodafuckingthunkit? And yet I smile

POEMS

Benderskum, Walden, Or A Different Drumbeat?

There once was a man who lived in the woods
He lived very simply for he knew that he could
Life was not easy to live in that manner
But being astute he was always a planner
Fetching wood for the fire and water and food
Clothes on his back and feet mostly shoed
The wonders of nature never ceased to amaze
Soft touch of the rain and the suns warming rays
On winter mornings his clothes often frozen
However it pleased him this life that he'd chosen
This wonderful life in amongst all the trees
At night time a candle to help him to see
The only buzzing was the sound of the bees
Or the hoot of an owl or the song of the breeze
He lived his life freely and as rich as a king
He didn't have money but what joy can that bring
His freedom was something that many have lost
For many have needs that are heavily embossed
With all the I's all dotted and all the T's crossed
They pay for life with freedom an unseemly cost
He lived in a way that most have forgotten
In the civilised world with foundations quite rotten
So if you go to the woods try not to rush
Listen to nature it's really quite lush
And perhaps stop to think take a leaf from this book

6

If you can't see the future don't bother to look
What will be is not certain and not something to worry
So live in the present there is no need to hurry

A bender with me String in the woods

Ignore The Debate

Ignore the debate
Our heads on your plate
You know it won't wait
Because then it's too late
If the temperatures rising why does it feel colder?
Questions like that only make you feel bolder
Hide all of the truth in one of your folders
So at least you'll be popular with the major stockholders
Of misdirection you are obviously masters
Blatantly ignoring all the natural disasters
When the news is all faked by your friendly broadcasters
The efforts you make are like sticking plasters
97% of actual climate experts totally agree
And their expert knowledge is good enough for me
That global warming is happening and it's definitely human-caused
Did you take all that in or is your brain still on pause
There really isn't time to waste we must do something now
Or carry on as always with the usual disavow
Venice council voted down any possible climate change action
Just after that it flooded and it felt like a chain reaction
Almost as if this was Karma but it gives me no satisfaction
Did it become major news here? No! There were too many other distractions
Last year we had the beast from the east, and in summer it was too fucking hot
You must have all noticed the seasons have totally gone to pot
This year it flooded and it's bound to get much worse
But they'll carry on lying as usual, copy chapter and verse
Minimization, Omission, Restructuring, are just three of the ways that they lie
Catching them out doesn't work either as then it's just flat out deny

So because of these things we can't leave it to them they simply aren't to be trusted
The way they behave as if nothing is wrong we ought to be fucking disgusted
But don't listen to me I know nothing you see then pretty soon we're gonna blow it
And by then it's too late to fix our mistakes and it's over before you know it

Just Because I Did It

Just because I did it doesn't mean I'm guilty
 If the only thing I did was break some stupid fucking law
Just because I did it doesn't mean I'm guilty
I don't believe your lies I've heard them all before
Just because I did it doesn't mean I'm guilty
I've watched your prohibition and the problems that it brings
There are puppets that will follow you but you'll never pull my strings
Just because I did it doesn't mean I'm guilty
That's only if I'm accepting your very crooked rules
I break them because they are based on lies, don't take me for a fool
You make them up to keep us down and say we are to blame
Whilst all along you feather your nest you really have no shame
Just because I did it doesn't mean I'm guilty I really don't accept your very broken law
Your choice seems to be to perpetuate the lies, so you're guilty and so much more
There are floods and famine and mass extinction the planet needs a hand
But there is a plant that can help a lot. What part don't you understand?
You hide behind the war on drugs the war that you've clearly lost
But it's all just smoke and mirrors, see? You continue to ignore the

cost
You act as if you've won this war but in reality you are losing
The police have previously upheld your law but some have started choosing
The world is in trouble and needs a break
But all you do is take, take, take
Climate crisis, global warming whatever term you choose
If we don't do something pretty soon we'll all just fuckin lose
There'll come a time when people wake and see what you are doing
But carry on with your lies and then see what us Prols are brewing
You saw the changes we were making and started to feel the fear
So last November made announcement for the entire world to hear
That for people with certain conditions cannabis was legal
I smelled out that lie straight away without the help of a beagle
But I don't just fight for medicine or at least not that alone
I fight for my world that you are stripping bare right down to the fucking bone
You seem to believe there's a Planet B and you will not be affected
When the shit hits the fan you'll soon find out that everything is connected
So step down off your gilded perch and listen to some sense
Or wait until it all falls apart with no time for recompense
Just because I did it doesn't mean I'm guilty when I refuse to follow your selfish fucking law
I follow my morals unlike yourselves you are rotten right to the core

If you know a benderskum you probably know it likes to get high, it was pretty high on this day back in 2010

Sowf Ov Lundern By String

Sometimes people ask me; 'Where are you from'?
And of course my usual reply is Sowf ov Lundern
Cos I'm not from those other really exotic places
I've only ever dreamed about with all their airs and graces
Huge castles posh houses big cities and towns
That I'm sure are really out there but I have never found
That the poles do exist I can only suppose
That may people went there once and actually froze
You know the north with its Eskimos and of course the polar bears

And igloos and Frost giants and ooh! Now I'm scared
Anyway then there's the West Country in a place that's known as
the West
I know they've got a great railway but little of the rest
And then where else is there? McScotty's Land right there at the
top
To get there you start walking today and a few weeks later stop
I'm not really certain if it's really above or below the north
But I've heard with a car and a bucket of petrol it's easy to get back
and forth
Then the pole itself, that's if it really exists
Not a metaphorical stick just made up in a myth
And Wales though I can't really be certain if it is where it's drawn
on my map
The map was drawn by my best mate 'oody so blame him if it's
wrong or crap
There aren't any polar bears there or so I have been told
Although what I'm thinking right this second never ever gets old
I'm almost sure I've read somewhere that it rains almost all of the
year
And there are dragons flying everywhere though exciting a thing
to be feared
Every time the sun starts to shine daffodils just spring from the
ground
And the people only eat lumps of coal their wise men dig from the
ground
That dragon bit, though I've a feeling may be born of a trip
Also that people don't really eat coal oh yeah and the daffodil bit
You may now have sussed this out I'm useless at Jography
Because I didn't listen in school because it was far too boring for
me
To be honest I didn't listen then and I'm still not listening now
Running around with some headphones on can teach you about
maps and stuff. Really tell me how?
How to learn where everything is you'd have to see for yourself
And unless you can run really fucking fast leave that shit on the

shelf
But anyway it isn't possible to run across the sea
That's why it never happened, you just can't disagree
Now what was I saying? Errr oh yeah I think that there is a sea
That separates this bit from that bit in the map its plain to see

And then there's an island called Eye Land I think
A mythical land where dark beer's all they drink
They grow fields of shamrocks whatever they are
I hear you can get there by bridge in a car?
The bridge was built by a fat bloke called Johnson who I hear is a bit of a dick
He treats everybody with contempt and thinks that they're all thick
But to me everywhere is exotic cos I have never been
Even as far as Lundern to see the bluddy queen
Though the Sowf isn't really where I'm from or so I've always been told
Other places still existed and benderskum was made there in the dark, dark days of old
I first met up with it in a place called Batu Gajah
Which doesn't really exist I think unless its far, far, far
But how far that is seems to be a conundrum
Cos it's not on my map of the Sowf ov Lundern
I have a map of everyfink but it still ain't very clear
If there's an edge to everyfink if that place is there, there or here

Up Norf

I'm sure that you're all unawares
Of how scared I am of polar Bears

And then not to mention Eskimos
Coming this far north I expected to be froze
But I guess with climate change everywhere is skewiff
So the best thing I can think of is smoke a little spliff
Or maybe a phatty or a pipe or a bong
Get me really stoned and I might sing a song
Actually no forget that last statement
Or I'll probably get done for noise abatement
But what I will do like it or not

Digitised Homogenised Balls Of Paper

Balls of screwed up paper on the writer's floor
Balls of screwed up paper we don't see that no more
Balls of screwed up paper in the writers bin
Digitised homogenised now let the fun begin
Is it really, really real without an old typewriter
Can they say with hand on heart they really are a fighter

With reams of wasted paper before it made the writer think
Digitised homogenised magnetic fucking ink
Remember the balls of paper the writer left before
At least we now don't waste the trees we hear ecologists roar
Digitised homogenised cut and paste that phrase
No balls of wasted paper like in the good old days

However that's another lie the good old days I mean
Making us wish for a better world but one that has never been
History is relative to whoever wrote it down
You never wore a robe of silk it was just a tattered gown
No army ever conquered and put all wrongs to right
The truth is convoluted and black is truly white

These days though it's different live streaming across the world
See it as it's happening new future history being unfurled

Digitised homogenised only seconds for them to censor
Still in control but occasionally truth slips through the news dispenser
Digitised homogenised long gone the days of splendour
So photographic truth is gone replaced by the great pretender

All for one and one for all the musketeers once said
Nowadays its selfie time and chivalry is dead

I'll help you but first please pose with me for my audience online
If not good luck and my best wishes I'm sure you will be fine

Digitised homogenised it's all just magnetic fucking ink
Unlike the balls of paper when a writer still had to think

Poetry (Honestly)

Poetry written way back when
Poetry written with a pen
Poetry with feather dipped in ink
Poetry that almost makes you think

Poetry with themes so long forgotten
Poetry not born but still begotten
Poetry not really quite mundane
Poetry some different some the same

Poetry that really doesn't end
Poetry that really doesn't send
Poetry to soothe a battered heart
Poetry beginning at the start

Poetry not just to be poetic
Poetry that sometimes seems prophetic
Poetry that takes you for a ride
Poetry whose words you can't abide
Poetry that's just some words that rhyme
Poetry that wastes your valuable time
Poetry that's just a waste of space
Poetry that puts you in your place

Poetry that just goes on and on

Poetry without a real foundation
Poetry to heal the human nation
Poetry without any justification
Poetry or verbal procrastination

A benderskum got up one day ready to break his fast
Just like the many other times he'd done this in the past
He opened the fridge door to help decide the thing that he should eat
Being a vegan he obviously didn't see anything vaguely like meat
He did however see some mushroom a medley of a certain variety
Instantly he knew he was very soon saying goodbye to normal sobriety
Luckily though in isolation there was no real propriety
And nobody around to see him or cause any form anxiety
He would embark on a journey but not for the usual outward travel
But inward with a swirl as his mind begins to gradually unravel
A journey that would never be completed
A journey where all knowledge is secreted
Somewhere to find somewhere to lose
Some left behind if that's what you choose
This place you can choose to leave or remain
This place you aren't quite mad and definitely not quite sane
But back to the fridge and it starts with some shrooms
To unlock the deepest of those hidden rooms
It's there he goes to look at the things he's going to paint
So from his imagination is something that they ain't
The stuff he scribbles he's actually seen and you could see them too
And just because he made this up it doesn't mean it isn't true

Fear The Purple

The sky was blue
You were safe you knew
Then the sky turned black
Must be ready for attack
So you step into the green
Where you think you can't be seen
But, what's that, up ahead?
A torchlight? But in red
You wish the sky was still the blue
When you were safe and this you knew
Now worried you dread to think
As the torchlight turns to pink
What the fuck will you do?
If the light instead of blue
Turns PURPLE
Because nothing rhymes with purple
But slightly more of a worry
I'll tell you in a hurry
Nothing rhymes with Orange or Silver
Nevertheless
Fear the Purple

HOW TO GET A
GIRLFRIEND

So I found this old recipe in a grimoire in the vault under my mansion, now I wasn't really looking to hook up with anyone but I'm a sucker for science. So if there's a choice to be made of just ignoring it as usual rather than waste the opportunity of a proper, pukka gen, no fucking about, scienfuckingtific experiment, I'm your guy, so I ignored it Later that day busy cutting up the victi...neigh...dinner, I got a telephone call from Istanbul advising me

1) never trust a man in a blue trench coat &
2) never drive a car when you're dead

It put me off, the dogs caught the scent of the nosh, then almost before I could react with the taser it was scoffed, greedy fuckers those mutts. No worries plenty more where they came from, but what was that again, I mean a blue trench coat is that even a thing?   Oh yeah the recipe;

To be desired by women It is necessary to take the heart of a virgin pigeon and have it swallowed by a viper: the viper will die because of the emblem of virtue and innocence that is the pigeon, whilst it is it is emblem of voice and calumny; therefore the viper will die in a more or less long time; then take her head, make it dry until it has no more smell, then crush it in a mortar with the double of hemp seed and drink the powder that will come from it in a glass of wine of four years, to which you will have mixed a few drops of The opium extract known under the name of 'laudanum'; then your complexion will become radiant, your lips rosy, and all women will desire you whatever your age

((Flamel 1842)Liber420:Cannabis,Magickal Herbs and the Occult)

Anyway what happened in the experiment was my skins first became radiant, then fluorescent then translucent then it all fell off and I've only just managed to sew enough bits salvaged from victi...neigh...meals to cover me tender raw bits And needless to say I didn't end up with a new partner in crime The laudenum was nice though

SCRIBBLES

1 - 5 photos by Darren Rigby with thanks
Therest photomagraphed by a benderskum
1) The memory of a Free Festival
2) Old Shoes and Picture Postcards
3) The big Book of Stuff
4) Hope
5) Save Ya Machine
6) Spiralino
7) Raindogs
8) Love Conquers all but nothing lasts forever
9) 9th and Hennepin
10) Jazz Police
11) Universal Pipe of Peace
12) Intrerspectivation
13) Bayeaux Selfestrie
14) Singapore
15) #thefake
16) The Dream

Satori must be something just the same
Or maybe just a little bit insane

Either way there's nonsense in my brain
Need to go to Barcelona, Spain
Or maybe back to Amsterdam, again
Eat vegan pancakes at a place in Waterlooplein
And get Rosie and Riffy cheese again
Cashew Camembert I would not refrain
It's too fucking nice and I'm not insane
I've been left unsupervised so I'm not the one to blame
Some people think me wild but I'm really very tame
a couple of short bits with scribble backgrounds

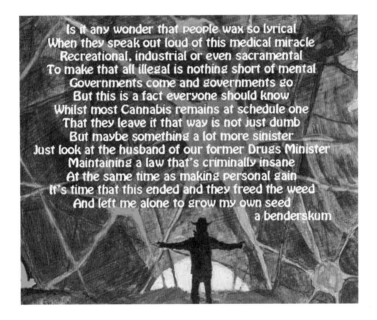

Cannabis, poetry and activism seems a strange combination
Although they fit really well during herbal castration
Obsolete laws quite in need of cessation
Make smoking a spliff more than mere assignation
Start to make sense then you'll cause celebration
Cannabis, poetry and activism seems a perfect combination
a benderskum

What he said

Is it any wonder that people wax so lyrical
When they speak out loud of this medical miracle
Recreational, industrial or even sacramental
To make that all illegal is nothing short of mental
Governments come and governments go
But this is a fact everyone should know
Whilst most Cannabis remains at schedule one
That they leave it that way is not just dumb
But maybe something a lot more sinister
Just look at the husband of our former Drugs Minister
Maintaining a law that's criminally insane
At the same time as making personal gain
It's time that this ended and they freed the weed
And left me alone to grow my own seed
a benderskum

SNOWY THE BUSKER

Back in the early 90s maybe 1992/3 or thereabouts I used a homeless day centre, occasionally to get a bath, I mostly didn't eat there for two reasons not the least of which was the terrible food they served. I was even really unpopular with their cook when I wrote in the suggestions book that a vegetarian alternative that wasn't just; cabbage, carrots and potatoes would be a healthier choice. When asked by the manager if I would make a picture for a Christmas card I replied I don't really do Christmas but I don't mind making a card for you. So as it only meant making a scribble, I made a snowman busking with a hat in front of him with some money in it next to a sign that said spare some change for the homeless at Christmas, in pen and ink, really simple hardly any lines. When I gave them the scribble ten minutes later they looked embarrassed then told me, they couldn't use it as the card was begging actually asking for money. Which was of course nonsense but nevertheless how it really is for independent charities that try to help out with homelessness. I wanted to help them out so I said ok no worries screwed up the scribble and put it in the bin. and made and a second card with a snowman busking with a hat with some money in it I next to a sign that said spare a thought for the homeless at Christmas they said they could use that because it wasn't asking for money.

Well that was up to them I didn't really care they had lots of Christmas cards printed and loads of the people that went there homeless people and people who lived in flats and whatever that always hang around at homeless centres started selling it some kept the money and got pissed some handed it in for the funding I'm not sure what it they used it for but I didn't really care. I was invited to the launch it was to be held in the Guildhall as part of the Lord Mayor's Christmas fund raising blah, blah, blah, and yeah it is the Lord Mayor because it's Canterbury. So they said to me come along at 4 o'clock (maybe I don't know, or I can't remember I'm just making up the time) to this meeting it's a council meeting in the Mayors Chambers in the Guildhall, Pomp and Splendour, anyway I'd decided I wasn't going because... Well, just fuck all that shit. One of my mates Mental Mick an acid dealer (well he was at least that week) really wanted me to definitely go, to represent us street people apparently, which cracked me up, I told him 'no not my thing dude', so he offered me two trips if I went.

Well I've always been a bit of a sucker for nice acid and his stock at that point was Purple Heart microdots which were the absolute don. So what could I do but accept his kind offer with a thank you and hand them over then. Before he gave them to me he said 'you can't take them before you go', so I said 'alright then I won't but you gotta give them to me now', because I know you, you'll sell them otherwise, so he said 'yeah alright then but remember you can't take them before you go'. So a bit reluctantly he gave them to me and I immediately unwrapped and swallowed them to which he said 'you bastard you said you weren't going to take them before you go. I answered 'I'm not going yet I'm not going for a while' he replied 'what are you gonna do then' 'Enjoy the ride' I told him, so I wandered up and down the town oblivious to what was going on around me, scribbled a bit while the world turned in spirals at least from where I was observing it. At some point some bloke came and told me oh it's time for you to go to this thing I think my mate had sent him because he was convinced I wouldn't go, to be honest it was quite a low priority and I'd already forgotten. Mick was certain I was a good representative although of what I've never been really sure as I was just a tramp like everybody else in my circumstances. Anyway off I went to the Guildhall tripping my tits off, when I arrived I couldn't find a door because there is not a door where I was looking it was accessible from the boneyard next door (boneyard is a churchyard with graves in case you didn't know). I was tripping happily walking along the outside wall then back again when suddenly two little old ladies who helped as volunteers at the day centre and soup kitchens and suchlike, grabbed my arm and said 'hello Rocky' so I assumed they obviously knew me 'are you lost?' they asked 'yes, I can't find the door' I replied 'That's because it's not here, come with us we know the way', so off we went through the boneyard to the entrance door they went to put their coats up. Well I was giving nobody my coat it had too many valuable things in the pockets of course all tramp treasure or in other words; rubbish. As a tramp I always had pockets full of crap I think at the time I had somewhere in the region of about 20 pockets it felt like the more pockets I had the more important I was, in my own head. Anyway as I walked in the door, a waiter came up who I thought was a penguin any squeaked at me 'Stibbledibbledibsup' which frankly I didn't understand and thought it must be some secret penguin language. However it turned out he was offering me stilton wheels whatever they are, strangely enough I didn't want one when I figured it out they sounded disgusting so I said 'no give me proper food or just fuck off out my face'. Just then another penguin came and offered me a glass of wine to which I declined with 'no I don't drink and I don't want your poxy wine, I would rather have some cold water I don't suppose you've got any of that in your pockets do you he waddled off as penguins do squawking about something about not carrying water round in his pockets. I said 'well nor do I' pulling my empty plastic water bottle from my pocket and 'it's just not good enough' at that point the mayor came along and introduced himself 'hello I'm the mayor are you Rocky and I said 'yes I am, mostly because I am' he asked me what the problem was. I told him his penguins, assuming they were his, won't get me any water. He said come with me to my private chambers although I thought it sounded a tad dodgy I thought I could probably handle myself if he tried to get frisky. So off we went into his private rooms and told me to help myself as he had plenty of water in the taps, for which I was grateful. He wanted me to tell him how is how difficult it was being on the streets so I pointed out at that moment I wasn't on the street but there in his private Chambers to which he said 'oh yes very droll' the sort of stuff posh people usually said to people like me. Anyway happy that I had some cold water he asked 'do you not drink alcohol'? No I replied I smoke weed and do acid which he probably didn't understand to be fair. I do drink, but only water or coffee if it isn't instant, but water is really hard to get at night if you don't have anywhere to live because in the night toilets they only have warm water and it's disgusting to drink, so if you want to do something useful do something about that. He said he would look into it, yeah right. It was then time to go and get on with the blah, blah, blah, it turned out it was a proper council meeting with all the rigmarole that entails, paper shuffling people, coughing and stuff, There was I sitting amongst it all and I noticed something on my boot is broken so forgetting where I was because I was tripping my tits off very loudly I exclaimed 'Fuck my things broken' so I bent down to fix it, a while later when I looked up it had all gone quiet and everybody was looking at me so I told them it was fixed and they could carry on with it, so get on with it they did, odd they waited for me, nice of them too. When it all finished I was wandering around in this big room trying to work out what all the food was and if t was poisonous or not, then eventually deciding that it was all probably inedible. Then a reporter from the local lie rag came to talk to me asking me all these strange questions about homeless issues which I had no idea about whatsoever, stuff like how did I feel about people spending a night out in the cold to show solidarity with the likes of me. I had no idea what she meant at the time but it seems people all buddy up in their sleeping bags and blankets and spend the night out in the cold probably praying or something to make homeless people feel better. I wish I'd known it might have made me feel better, although to be honest I didn't really feel too bad most of the time; the drugs and the fact that I was half crazy helped though. She asked where I lived 'I told her that when I managed to walk the seven miles to get there I lived in a caravan with no roof and no windows, deep in some woods way out of town, it was nice I liked it people left me alone'. She said 'oh no, that's terrible, I'll tell you what I'll get you a doggy bag of food' I told her 'no, no it's fine, it's okay' but she insisted and got this stuff together. Then we went out into the Westgate gardens next to the river and sat on a bench in this turret thing part of the old city wall that sticks out into the river from the gardens. I wanted to sit and have a spliff she followed and sat down next to me. I'm not really sure why but a very strange thing then happened suddenly she tried to snog me. This seemed really odd and I decided that I was probably her bit of rough for the evening anyway, as she was obviously quite posh and fairly pretty. I managed to get her to stop and not try to snog me anymore because I didn't want it and then she said alright well let's get on with the interview then I said okay. Looking back I realise it was probably my fault because I vaguely remember saying when asked for a quote something like 'I think you're really horny' but I can't actually remember whether that was before she tried to snog me, or after but as I said I was tripping. She eventually left I'm not really sure when but she left the bag of disgusting with me that I fed to the swans. I went home to wherever I was staying at the time 'home sweet homeless' often at that point it was the derelict old police station a good dry place that the posers hadn't yet found and fucked up, although not all the rooms were nice, the cells were particularly horrible to sleep in or at least weird anyway. Next morning I went to the town I got my breakfast at the homeless centre and the reporter from the evening turned up having come to interview the staff she saw me came and said 'hello' and wanted to talk about my quote from last night, 'I don't think I can print it' so I asked 'what are you talking about' and she told me the one where I thought she was horny 'Oops' I said and started laughing because it was quite funny and she got very, very cross with me and stormed off to be fair she wasn't very horny but then I didn't really do that sort of thing anyway. I had been celibate for a while and I only ever got horny when I was tripping Bad, bad benderskum.

The centre did however make well over £500 in profit from the sale of Christmas cards that year. Still not sure what it was used for I know all the staff and volunteers had a meal in a local restaurant as a Christmas treat.

A few months later I tried to get a loan of twenty five quid to buy some trousers as mine were more patch and holes than actual clothing but they refused, too late for me to get any Christmas cards to sell too.

OH NO MORE
BLOODY POEMS

This

If you've ever been so stressed that you can't just chill and smoke
And your very best companion's is an artificially intelligent bloke
And the world you know can only be described as a very unfunny joke
And you need to keep away from each other to ensure that you don't croak
And the people in charge haven't a clue
Although neither do I and nor do you
This is something entirely new
Genetically modified chemical stew
One day on a future TV show they'll ask someone in a quiz
Was it that bloody virus thing and would you call it the shiz?
Everything seems to be following a script it could be on television
And then after all it is what it is don't look for guidance from politicians
Spreading itself unseen, unheard the epitome of stealth
Steadfastly it is after the denigration of our health
Billionaires take notice it cares not for your wealth
Some are even saying that none of this stuff is true
Because every year people die from the common or garden flu

Feel free to have that opinion it makes no odds to me
But ask me to agree with your opinion get back in the sea
But social isolation isn't too bad for me
With String and Woody the model I'm in perfect company
There was a lone and loony man that nobody could believe
Then he became the organ grinder with a monkey up his sleeve

Then from the east came a queen with a body all covered in spikes
Her intention was to put a stop to the things that everyone likes
The only ways to stop her is stay at home and hide
And get yourself a hazmat suit if you wish to go outside
But that is just me scare mongering I doubt it'll come to that
But if it does I'm gonna smoke the herb that turns folk into bats
Bill Hicks said it doesn't matter because it's all just a ride
But I wanted to be a lumberjack with my faithful dog at my side

Me "Excuse me ossifer but I think somebody here is breaking the law."
Popo " Oh yes sir and what law might that be."
Me " That shit law that makes no sense, you know where Cannabis is Schedule !, meaning it has no medicinal value. Giving your lot the right to kick people's doors in"
Popo "Well does it have medicinal value?"
Me "According to the government, yes as they legalised it for medicinal use on November 1st 2018"
Popo "I don't think I read that memo."

A Strange Poem

Strange to be normal when everything's weird
Strange that reality is all that we feared
Stranger than fiction, weirder than fact

Stranger than actors that simply, can't act
trangely strange but oddly normal
trangely naked while trying to be formal

Strange that I scribble cos I simply can't paint
trange you believe that I'm something i ain't
trange that to breathe becomes such a task

Strange it's ignored when I ask, ask and ask
trange days are here and we've waited so long
trange that an anthem is merely a song

Strange that the words were all simply wrong
trange I'm so weak when I used to be strong
trange to believe that we're not in great danger

Strange in the mirror there is only a stranger

Stop, Get The Fuck Out Of Your Car,

take off your shoes and walk on the land

The hard times are coming it's hard to deny
Look at the climate look at the sky
Eventually they'll cut down most of the trees
And the ones that are left will be full of disease
Thousand of species will go extinct every year
But the average citizen still doesn't care
There'll be Flora museums and Fauna zoos
When the natural has gone and nothings renewed
With their GM seeds they'll try to grow food

But with GM seeds plantings too crude
Those seeds need the chemicals made out of oil
They were never designed to grow just in soil
But there will soon be no oil even for cars
Unless they discover a supply up on Mars
With the air too polluted and food really short
They'll look to the pasts ignored lessons taught
By then it's too late and there's no turning back
Too late to fix it or pick up the slack

There will still be roads from this place to that
But no life in sight not even a cat

Stockholm Syndrome 2

Did you ever believe what they told you?
Did you ever believe what they said?
Did you ever believe when they said that quite soon?
Millions of you might well be dead
I'm not really sure how they got there
Except democracy's a bit of a joke
They said wash your hands and carry on
But try not to cough or to choke
The world just went crazy for bog roll
And pasta and lentils and rice
But lucky for me I'm a vegan
So apparently think cardboard tastes nice
Luckily the magic money tree flowered
Just about in the nick of time
So everyone says the buffoon is ok
And will probably save us from dying
For he's got it himself and still soldiers on
To lead us astray yet again

At the rate we are going our daily count
Will soon exceed Italy and Spain
With a team of experts and a cobra meeting
Out in the fields the sheeple are bleating
Or staying indoors but it's terribly hard
Especially without a garden or yard
So this puts the popo on high alert
So away from real crime they must divert
What sort of crime? You know growing a plant
Some plants are ok to grow, some though you can't
I'm not saying it's impossible just that it's a crime
And if the popo catch you, you may well do time
But that is a very big digression
From the point of this blah, blah, blah, poetry session
Now back to the country and I'm still being kind
When I say 'Stockholm Syndrome' comes to mind
They aren't in it for you and I don't want to squabble
Just take a deep breath, give your head a wobble
We've had years of austerity and been cut to the quick
Yet still they are there our demockeracy is sick
I keep seeing reports about wasted fresh food
Thrown in landfill bins now isn't that rude
Or maybe the next step of human evolution
Homo-Consumerus the final solution
When the shelves are all empty and there's nothing to buy
They'll all look again at that funny blonde guy
Then he'll make those promises he'll never keep
And you'll all believe him like good little sheep
So 'Stockholm Syndrome' gets a mention once again
Because that odd expression is flashing in my brain
But there are some things that you can do
To make yourself free and they're nothing new
Be kind, be truthful be good of heart
That's the best way to make a start
Being nice and kind does not make you weak
And you don't have to turn the other cheek

Don't worry over things that are out of your hands
Be your own destiny make your own plans
No, do as you're told by the powers that be
I'm just a benderskum don't listen to me

Now

The people of Earth are down on their knees
While the monsters in charge do what they please
The psychopath governments worse than disease
Born on your lips or borne on a breeze
If they don't like our actions they just change the law
They think we are stupid but they're bad to the core

They leave the vulnerable to die on their own
While powerless monarchs on golden thrones

Allow them autonomy cos they're bad to the bone
It makes me so angry and I'm not all alone
When the world is run by faceless people old and grey
And they don't allow freedom so there's nothing to say

It's time for a change let it soon be the day
Don't listen to me find your own way
There's only one world for all of humanity
Whilst they still act as if there's a planet B
I used to believe we had democracy
But now it's obvious it's just hypocrisy
Certainly no choice in this autocracy

Our world is in crisis it couldn't be worse
We have to do something that's chapter and verse
We cannot afford this system of use, use, use
Because if we continue we can only lose
I never agreed to live like a serf
And neither did you for what it's worth

There are things we can do to make it get better
But that's not a petition or an overlooked letter
I hear people say I can't make a change
An attitude I've always thought very strange
'I'm only one person I can't do it alone,
So I'll sit and stare at my mobile phone'

You could get up and do it don't sit and moan
The time is now the seeds have been sown
Before it's too late and the chance has been blown
You may think that it cannot done
But the battle is now and it has to be won

Stop buying shit that you simply don't need
Get out in the garden and plant some seed

We are all to blame there is no acquittal
Start right away little by little

Inch by inch it's a cinch
Yard by yard it's bloody hard

There are over 6 billion in the human race
So let's not trip over let's tie that lace
And soon enough I'm sure that we'll see
There's still a world left for you and me

Not In The Public Interest

The Crown Prosecution Service have decided it's not
In the best public interest to prosecute for pot
Or if you want me to put it another way
That's the news we heard from Carlisle today
So I presume it's no longer considered a crime
To indulge in some favourite habits of mine
However don't forget all the worry this caused
While the popo just follow these broken laws
Which gives them the right to break down our doors
Or because it is broken it ought to be paused
And that they could without any delay
Pause the law I mean right here and now today
Then they'll have more time to squabble and squabble they certainly will
Because losing face to politicians is the bitterest of pill
But Lezley and Mark are two heroes of mine, how dare they break

down their door
The result was the same in this unfunny game that it was when they did it before
So the law hasn't changed and to them it's a game
In this land where our government like snorting cocaine
So this is the law as far as I can see
That if I did certain things I'd be acting illegally
Production, possession or distribution of cannabis
But not actually the plant which just takes the piss
This is the place this makes my brain go and I won't even apologize
The seed is still legal so while looking at mine I dropped it and just did not realise
It grew into a plant with no help from me and became a sight to see
And being a gardener as I've been for a while I love to eat fresh growing leaves
I also eat flowers straight from a plant without even using my hands
So none of those illegal actions would have happened I'm sure you understand
What I'm trying to say is it's all about words
An unfunny joke and frankly absurd
They're not giving up yet and still try to maintain this facade of law and order
And if it means it's ok in Carlisle it should be the same right across the border
This battle was won now I hope Mark and Lezley can at least for a little while rest
Oh! Did I tell you before they're heroes of mine and what I call two of the best
But this war is not over even though they are losing
We need to remember what we should be choosing
That legalisation is not what it seems
Let me explain you may see what I mean
Luxembourg I hear has legalised

Remove 5 letters it sounds like lies
Canada has thirty-seven and a half million citizens and legalising seems done and dusted
But with less than four hundred legal selling points any others will really get busted
Uraguay although smaller I believe is the same,
Although, I quite like what I heard they are doing in Spain
So legalisation isn't the way it's a lie with a new set of rules
And yet they still peddle that same tired mantra in reality they do think we're fools
Decriminalise, and deschedule cannabis is a better route I feel
Because with legalisation there'd be a new set of rules just like re-inventing the wheel
I'm not talking of quality and quantity control that is a quite different fight
This is for freedom to be a herbalist as a basic human right
Leave me alone
I'll grow my own
Or if I manage to grow enough
I'll pass it along like I do with most stuff
Anyway back to my heroes I'm glad that bits now done and dusted
And whatever you do I hope that you will never again get busted
Cannamaste

HOW WAS I EVER
IN THE ARMY

When I was 17 years old I got stuck in the army more of how that occurred later needless to say I wasn't meant to be there and hated every minute of it One night I went out with a mate I called grandad because he was 25 and at 17, he knew so much more than me so seemed like an ancient wise man. He'd invited me to come to the Rag and Oil Corps Club Disco I said yeah so off we went to this strange place which was a Scottish club, whatever that means. We arrived before the doors opened and were standing outside waiting. He asked me if I knew what acid is. I said 'what do you mean like the drug' he replied 'yeah the drug LSD' I said that I'd heard of it but never tried it. He then asked if I'd like to try some to which after a long half a second asked 'What? When? Now? 'Yeah' he said 'I've got some' So I said 'okay let's give it a go, what do I do' He then handed me this paper thing a bit smaller than a postage stamp with four orange suns printed on it. He told me I must fold in four and tear it, then swallow it . So that's exactly what I did apart from I didn't hear him say tear it so I so I swallowed all of it it. He looked at me and asked if I'd just swallowed all of it? and added that he only meant for me to take a quarter of it but it was okay as he had plenty more anyway. Then laughed and said 'enjoy your trip'. Then the place opened and we went in and he got me a beer, I sat down with my beer in front of me and in a short while, maybe about half an hour or so, I thought I was inside a pinball machine. Bangs noises and things going on which was I suppose the disco playing in the background but I was tripping and I thought that the world had transformed into a huge pinball machine and then it all became more and more bizarre. There were all these skinheads because it was the army and all I could see were ears everywhere ears, ears, ears and more ears. Furthermore I thought all of these skinheads were driving around in Cadillacs inside the pinball machine and bouncing off the bumpers with their cars but it was actually just people dancing and the music was noisy. I think at about 11 o'clock my full pint of beer still in front of. I was still dripping my tits off but had to go back to the barracks room where I slept sort of in a very multicolour night. The next morning I'm still tripping my tits off and I had to go on parade and I couldn't be bothered to shave first, so I took my little battery shaver with me that. I decided to start shaving when I grew bored standing there gazing at the amazing universe. I forgot I was on parade when suddenly a Sergeant major was in front of me steam pouring out of his ears and his nostrils and screaming at me something I didn't really understand. Actually I just laughed at him and said you're not even real fuck off get out my face then I was frogmarched away and locked up. Very soon I was given polish a dustbinn and a toothbrush after a while I became quite good at polishing dustbins. Actually it wasn't just dustbins that week I had to dig a trench I think it was about 20 metres long 1 1/2 metres wide and a metre deep it took me all week to dig it by myself. Then at the end of the week it was the weekend (odd how that happens) so I went and did what I normally didgot off my tits which is what you do as a teenager especially in the 1970s it's probably the same even now too I guess. The following week I was in just as much trouble as before, it didn't really matter I didn't really care but my new job for that week was to fill in the 20 metres long trench and level it all off and put new turf on it. When I was finished doing that because that didn't take a week it was back to polishing dustbins. I also had to paint some stones white and then some other inane tasks that wee designed to do my nut in and break my spirit. But you know what? I didn't really give a toss, I should not have been there, I didn't have a green brain, so couldn't take it seriously and they should have just thrown me out it would've been more sensible.

Whilst in Osnabruk, Germany I made some really good friends local Germans at rock 'n' roll bar some proper nutbars. There is a guy called Elvis with blond hairhis was nickname was Elvis but he had punk look nothing like Elvis he was crazy had a loaded pistol he was always waving Had two really good mates Ted and Maggie, Ted was English and had been in the army but stayed there in Germany after he came liked it there and his girlfriend Maggie she was absolutely stunning and she had an identical twin sister Marina (they looked kind of like Amy Winehouse) she hung around with us but that's about all really, she was in love with this one eyed guy I don't even know what his name was rock 'n' roll singer. One one night we were in my favourite bar owned by a German friend called Uve, the bar was The Panorama Hard Rock Cafe and we sitting by the massive windows watching a massive fight in the Market Square below. It was between I presumed some paratroopers and gypsies lived on a huge site near the town it was very full on and there was a lot of blood everywhere and then at one point there were police, military police but people were still fighting, for ages including with the popo. Anyway later on in the evening I was sitting with Uve, Ted ,Maggie and Marina the German police came in with a gypsy guy. They were looking for someone wearing white shoes who had stabbed his friend. We didn't see the stabbing but like I said it was full on out there. The guy saw my feet up on the table wearing my white brothel creeper shoes, which I loved, he pointed at me and said he recognised me and I was definitely the one. Marina said no, no he's been sitting here with me all evening, put a arm round me and kissed me on the cheek. At which the guy lunged at her and started screamed at her and called her a lying slut in German, luckily the popo holding him dragged him back, threw him on the floor and then handcuffed him and left. Every night in that bar was very funny, It was the watering hole of an alternative scene, lots of my friends were prostitutes, pimps, criminals and pimps and just generally dodgy people and if you're in the army you weren't allowed in there. Uve as I said was my friend and as he owned the place it was up to him anyway, they all realised I wasn't actually a soldier even though I was in the army. About 2 o'clock every morning 2 am every night whatever you like to go to with morning, night I don't care, Uve would shout hey Rocky do you want some tea. I used to love my late night tea then then he would ask what flavour do you want maybe mango? Mango tea was the bollocks but then the stuff he had for teatime was the shit. It was funny in amongst all this mayhem with all this madness going on, all these dodgy people surrounding us andhe would come over with the tray a teapot 2 cups a bowl with sugar lumps in it never milk because that was always disgusting even then. One day in Osnabruk I came across an art gallery showing the work of one of my favourite artists Felix Nussbaum It was the first time I'd heard of him, his pictures were mostly surreal but his early work was more classisit and similar to the early works of Piccasso before he became a cubist. I've always loved that sort of stuff . Felix was a local guy who died in Auschwitz concentration camp his artwork was quite political and after he was sent to Auschwitz concentration camp they made him paint more and more but his paintings got very dark and very political but I don't think the people he was painting them for, the Nazis, fully understood what he was painting or he may have died sooner. I think he understood what was going on poor guy but his paintings are brilliant. I remember sitting one night at 6 in the morning it was it was nearly dawn I was due back in the barracks at 7 and I was sitting with Marina on a park bench outside the old city gates when a German popo car pulled up onto the pavement and the plod came over said 'Ausweiss' which meant identity card so I showed mine which was no problem but Marina who I think was about 19 only had this screwed up piece of paper that she was given when she left secondary school three years before. It was not really even legible anymore she said she had never ever gone and got a proper one as she was an anarchist and a free person. I do love anarchists but they took her away because you're not allowed to not have ID in Germany even then, they released her later but not before taking her to wherever they give out ID cards. Where I lived was an old Nazi headquarters at the top of a hill it was a castle but called Caprivi kaserne. I lived on about the seventh floor I think I woke up one morning and there was loads of noise nearby and I were round to have a look what was going on one of my mates was there and he had two of my prostitute friends in bed with him it was so funny he asked me if I wanted to join but I said I'm good I'll give it a miss cause it's not my sort of thing. I was soon due to leave the army, I should've left already but they stitched me up and made me stay longer as I 'd bought myself out I gave him £300 but about two years before I signed for more service so that it looks like I wanted to stay in for nine years which meant I got an extra hundred pounds a month in my wage packet so the two years I got paid an extra hundred pounds which meant incidentally I got paid £2,400 extra and paid them £300 to get out it was a good deal in my book. But I think they messed me about even cancelled my leaving and gave the money back, so I had to start the whole process again. I had gangrene in one of my arms, from a work injury, which I couldn't let them know about but had to have a medical when I left the army this is pretty much how it went. I had to be clean shaved otherwise I couldn't do my medical and I went into the room stand on their scales and state my weight, height cough you know the one, yeah you know cough and drop he looked in my mouth said yeah you're fine and that was it. I had to go to Arborfield in Berkshire to do that it was ridiculous I couldn't just leave where I was stationed, no, I had to get this out of the way place it was really difficult to get to and was only army people living there in those days I think it's quite a posh of area no no longer army but you know lots of places like that these days and then I was out and that was me done and dusted I try to get out on by first week my mate did it he he joined the army just the same he stayed in for five days and then left because you got five days grace in those five days if you didn't like it you could leave well in between him doing it and me trying the same thing they changed the system and where are you signed to say you would join the army when you signed to say you were joining the army was when the five day started I didn't go there for another two weeks. So when I tried it, no I couldn't do it I had to stay and that was a simple as that I asked when I can get out and they told me four years four fucking years. It actually turned out to be a 4 1/2 because they stitched me up. I was getting out in four years and then they posted me to a new place me not knowing how it worked so well I'm only going to be there a couple days what a waste of time when I got to the nearest place I hadn't shaved my uniform was as usual a bag of shit (wish it was had been) and this Sergeant Major started screaming at me and I said I don't care mate I'm out of here in a couple of days he said I don't think so sunshine you just got posted it means you're here for at least six months. I said I bought myself out he said that's cancelled because you came here which meant I had no longer bought myself out as I said they re-deposited the £300 into my bank and I had to go through the same old bullshit again had to see the colonel wearing my best uniform which was to be honest usually screwed up in the bottom of my kitbag bag most of the time so I had to press that and look all nice and smart my boots. I never ever polished my boots what a waste of time polishing your boots I used to paint them with black gloss paint every morning for parades so it looks like they were polished but if you touched them , well it was wet paint It's all good it was all a learning curve anyway it meant that I got to stay in this wicked castle right down in the main part of town I never went out of the gate because I probably would have had to sign out but then they'd know how long I was out for and it would've raised questions. I got some wire cutters and cut hole in the back fence it was only a chain link fence so I just made a new exit that I could climb out and I was in town it was brilliant loved it, well being in town. Not being in the army but the town was good and the people were great.

As for driving a tank on cannabis; well that was easy because it mostly drove itself and not very fast anyway.

Apart from once they got some new tanks, when we were just parked up at the edge of this I don't know dust bowl I suppose then all this convoy of staff cars arrived and then a deuce and a half (huge tank transporter lorry) came up with full of brand new shiny tanks with shiny paint on them. They drove one down off the back of the loader and parked it up, the officers all had a look around it clambering all over it then the whole entourage went off for lunch probably. They just left it I guess they thought it was safe as we were there so I guess they imagined we would look after it, Ha. I suggested to my commander who was also my mate, that we could race this new tank against our 434 and he wasn't really up for it I said I'll let you drive the full 434 and I'll drive that thing, he said but you'll get in so much trouble, I said yeah but I don't care I'm always in trouble so what's new so off we went. Then I sweetened it with a case of beer if he wins that did it. I said we'll go round that tree and back and the first one back is the winner. I don't even know what it was called the tank I mean began with S anyway had a jag engine in it and it was supposedly did 70 mph in forward or reverse, crazy stuff. Well we got to the tree going well I was in the lead and coming back I misjudged how much of a slant there was on the bank that I was turning round on and the bloody thing rolled over. So there I am upside down in the fucking tank my mates screaming I fucking told now we're in so much fucking trouble what we gonna do. I said don't worry we've got a crane on the side of the 434 we'll just put it back upright again, the tracks weren't broken miraculously. So we put some shackles on the thing and pulled it back onto its tracks drove it back to where it had been parked It looked almost as good as new but it was it was very, very scratched and a bit dented in places and then not the armour of course but radio box and the exhaust I think it's antennae was also bent in half, oops, so we drove off and denied ever being there. There's more of this army stuff but it's all as boring as this.

ME OLD MUCKER
BENDERSKUM

A Poem By String

The publisher of this book of utter drivel

Born in Malaysia

Skun up in a cave

It lived in a forest

It must be depraved

Strangled its son to teach him respect

Got really skinny but that's what you'd expect

When they gave it leukaemia to make it back down

That didn't work you can't make it frown

Its invisible friend is a great guy called String

Its life mantra is nonsense if that is a thing

It thinks that two heads are better than one

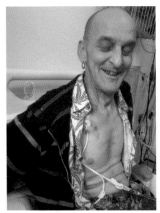

But a bone marrow transplant was not so much fun

It don't give a toss if you like it or not

As long as its world still supplies it with pot

It's just a benderskum and that's all It can be

Totally impervious I hope you will see

OH YES UNLUCKY
EVEN MORE POEMS

Purple

I do indeed wear purple some say a tad too much
I believe that's a matter of taste each to their own or such
I could also have worn orange but then I'd just look Dutch
Or perhaps a suit of silver but maybe that'd be too much
Either way I love my purple and nothing rhymes with it
Not even in my poems which I know are a little shit
Whenever I have people round did you guess I'm a cannibal
Whenever people visited I ate them one all all
As for reading papers I'm behind on current affairs
I don't like to read all that doom and gloom as if no one really
cares

The Beach V2

I try to be an honest bloke and mostly tell the truth
But having been around a little while I'm somewhat long in the
tooth
I live in a town that's on the coast and live quite near the sea
Because I really detest the beach it's not a place for me

It's true I really don't like it so every single day
I'd rather be in my garden and keep myself away
I guaranfuckingtee it you will never hear me say
Lets all go down and sit on the beach or maybe even lay

Very much like vampires I have to avoid the sun
So going out to sunbathe just doesn't sound like fun
And it's not because I'm scared or visually impaired
But my nostrils really flared the last time that I stared

At that litter covered beach

But you lot who seem to love the place
Like most of the rest of the human race
So tell me what is proper when you need to go to the loo?
Because when you are desperate what else can you do?
Shit in a box, or a garden or in the bloody sea
All of those as choices sound quite rough to me
The toilets should be opened I really do agree

But what you do because they're not just sounds quite rough to
me
I'm glad I don't like beaches and I never ever did
All my life I've felt that way ever since I was a kid

I heard that down in Bournemouth people left 12 tons of shite
That's proper nasty behaviour and it's really not alright

If you are one of these people I wonder how you think
To leave your crap all over the place for others to clear your stink

I know it isn't pleasant and you may think I'm a bore
But joining you lot on the beach for me there's no allure

I could go on and on and on and really start to preach

Or leave you with a tiny glimpse of why I don't like the beach

Corona, Corona The Government Owns Ya

There were lots of protests all across the world
About corrupted governments accusations being hurled
So to thwart this free thinking a new plan unfurled

In France we heard they had the yellow vests
Their government's policies were the worst not the best

Then a virus suddenly appeared in a market place in china
A way to stop the protesting world and a very dangerous definer

Then along came the people in their tin foil hats
Conspiracies on the cause was it this or maybe that
Some people said it was made in a laboratory
Some said it was copied from a little known horror story

That some blamed the Chinese was clearly defamatory
Announcement by world leaders were merely preparatory
Some said the governments were using it to take back their con-

trol
Estimations were in millions to be the final death toll

Some maybe suffocated by stockpiled bog roll
There were many mentions of thirty three
A number connected to the top of the tree
A Diophantine equation as hard as can be
A3 + B3 + C3 will equal thirty three
It is used a lot by Mason's and in sacred geometry

The virus they say was deliberately made and also has a patent
While the basis of truth is hidden from us the result however is
blatant
The anagram of corona virus turned out to be carnivorous
But it came from soup containing bat is just a bit ridiculous

That last sentence was very odd due to some of the words I will
bet
But finding a place in a rhyme for bot is something I haven't done
yet

So what can we do to make ourselves safe isn't the answer obvious
itself?
For a start don't go stockpiling stuff leave that shit on the shelf
Wash your hands is what seems expert advice
So everyone does it and doesn't think twice
Hanitizer sales have gone through the roof that stuffs never been
so popular
Remember though with that expert advice the importance of
seems as the copular
For they really don't know any more than you
The difference is scary because it's something new

Coronadebt

They called it yes they called it, they told us it was coming
But because of cuts it overtook we were walking it was running
At first they tried to convince us to build up herd immunity
Because if the vulnerable all died off it's a cash saving opportun-
ity
You may think they have your interests at heart
But they cocked it up right from the start

When you realise the government is lying to you that's called
apprehension
But if you think they have a bloody clue you haven't been paying
attention
There's a corona bloody virus and it's got us all locked down
The shops and things are mostly shut in every bloody town

On Thursday night the nation all went out to clap
But the way the government have handled this is just a pile of crap
Because of the thing called austerity the NHS are struggling
With the way this government have funded it they ought to take
up juggling

Every day on BBC they pretended to be clarifying
While the key workers on the front line had already started dying

They didn't have protective clothing or the equipment that they
need
The only reason that it was like that is privatised industry greed

And it's definitely gonna get loadsworse long before it's better
But don't worry folks cos your government is sending you an ex-
pensive fucking letter

They initiated a lockdown but didn't say it was mandatory
So thousands flocked to the beaches but that's another story
They told all the self employed they'd help them out in June
But that is about as much use then as howling at the moon
They got on the TV and blah, blah, blah'd about slowing the cor-
ona threat
But when it's done and dusted you'll owe them corona debt

So there I was in isolation thinking about this stuff
While the government try to spin another corona bluff

Coronaspiracies And A Tribute To;

"There's a one-eyed yellow idol to the north of Khatmandu,
There's a little marble cross below the town;
There's a broken-hearted woman tends the grave of Mad Carew,
And the Yellow God forever gazes down"
James Milton Hayes

Where did it come from what are they doing?
When it's done and dusted will civilisation be lain ruin?
Since before this virus appeared governments had become far seedier
And you'll scare the shirt right off your back believing social media
In the New World Order Coronaspiracies abound
Every day a new one makes our heads spin round
They made it in a laboratory but we know not who they are
The men behind the men behind or something as bizarre
It isn't real it's just a scam is what I hear folks say
But many people don't survive to see another day
It's all 5g I hear some say which makes me quite amused
Another pile of bullshit to make people Coronafused
Civilisation was starting to crumble they were fearful at the top
So the governments got together to make dissention stop
I can't believe the stuff I hear it spins my head around
But in the New World Order Coronaspiracies abound
But there is a really good side effect that isn't all that strange
The air is getting clearer is this Corona Climate Change?
Because the World's is virtually locked down very few planes and cars
And industry almost at a stop and restaurants, cafes and bars
Now many have been encouraged to become a neighbourhood snitch
And every time a car door slams a hundred curtains twitch
Then the governments award themselves another ten grand more

To sit at home like the heroes they are and fight this viral war
While people are literally penniless and food is getting short
Those with an extra ten grand payout can afford more coke to snort
So what could be the answer? I really wish I knew
But there's a one-eyed yellow idol to the north of Khatmandu,
There's a little marble cross below the town;
There's a broken-hearted woman tends the grave of me and you,
And the Yellow God forever gazes down.

From Scratch

Genetically modified designer vagina
Mass produced in a factory in china
But where can the average Joe buy one from
I would have thought it was wish dot com
Everyone said the potentials fantastic
But that's no surprise when you're fucking with plastic

Is what I say factual or mere metaphor
Or making stuff up just to exercise my jaw
So this is my process and for me it works fine
Maybe not your way but definitely mine
I go into blank mode and shut off my brain
And flush all the mundane shit right down the drain

But then when I'm ready I count down in colour
Then let that all go till its greyer and duller
Though the colour sequence is important it isn't to this rhyme
So we'll just leave that story hanging for another place and time
At this point I'm primed and the adventures begin
With no outside contact but mucho plenty within

And what I see when I arrive is what I'm going to paint
So made up in my imagination is something which it ain't
So out I come from that strange place
And come to rejoin the human race
The image is ready at least in my head
But my body refuses so I do this instead
Hopefully tomorrow my body stops shaking
So rather than rhyming it's scribbles I'll be making
The paint will be splashing instead of it spilling
And if you could watch I'm sure you'd be thrilling
You'd notice the paintbrush stab like it's killing
Though believe it or not that's me really chilling
If you believe it I know then that you too are willing
To believe in my hunger that this stuff is fulfilling
If you want me to stop this just pay me a shilling
And…it's done
Like before it was begun

Cash Freedom Or Digital Control

So next time you go shopping forget your paper money
Because these days shopping's a joke but one that isn't funny

They really want to have a world that buys things digitally
I'm not just saying local shops I'm talking globally

The things they could get away with in a cashless society
Would be something to add on top of their usual impropriety
There wouldn't be a black market if no one accepted cash
So where would the likes of me buy our cannabis flowers or hash

The homeless people on the streets would very soon be dead
Without begging for some money they'd have no daily bread
Money used to have some value when they had a gold reserve
Now it's just some numbers an illusion a mystery they preserve

So when you go out shopping to buy the things you need
Go to the places that accept your cash don't let these fuckers succeed
They say the virus gets passed on with money made of paper
Then try to give you a paper receipt the logic is as solid as vapour

No career politician would I trust as far as I could throw
It's just a career they're not in it for you a fact you ought to know
When one comes along with different ideas the sort that you could trust
They grab his or her reputation and throw it under a bus

They are secure in their power as they've held it for so long
We remember the term revolution but just as a word in a song

So what can we do? You would need to ask a cleverer person than me
When they hold the keys to the kingdom there is little autonomy

The keys to the kingdom is a metaphor for there isn't a kingdom lock
They obviously think they are shepherds and we are a sleeping flock

Divide And Fall, That Says It All

If you push this narrative you just sound absurd
When you say marijuana is a racist word
Or even that its prohibition derived
That makes my vomit build up inside
I've tried to explain to give you a clue
It appears though that this is what you must do
I have continued to explain or at least I have tried
That this sort of rhetoric is a way to divide
Now it's also the acronym CBD
It's a cannabinoid a fact which you can't disagree
Weed is a word given to plants that have simply grown out of place
A plant that isn't wanted by gardeners but that's just a matter of taste
When you pick on a word to make a point it's simply a disgrace
Another form of prohibition and very commonplace
So back to marijuana a really melodic word
Long before Anslinger it would have definitely been heard
It came long before but there's no need to panic
A Mexican word so it sounds quite Hispanic

It came to the attention of William Hearst
An early prohibitionist and one of the worst
He used it in papers to make them all sell
Just to vilify Mexicans and cannabis as well
Not a word he made up it was there long before
As a yellow journalist he knew the score
Although nowadays when folks still argue his side
They are all prohibitionists that I cannot abide
Just do some research find out for your self
Then put it in place at the back of the shelf
When you say it's from Anslinger or Hearst I feel scorn
It was known by Mexicans before they were born
Hearst was quite worried so he did an assessment
Believing that hemp would devalue his investment
Anslinger was given a high ranking job by the uncle of his wife
He made the word quite famous back when racism was rife
He used it quite derisively to make white folks feel contempt
So they didn't even realise he was talking of cannabis, hemp
A heavily invested banker wanted cannabis farming to stop
Popular Mechanics magazine called it a billion dollar crop
The banker I mentioned was Andrew Mellon invested in fossil oil
I imagine this crop where he wasn't invested probably made his
blood boil

So the love of my life I still call Mary Jane
If you can't see the truth I'll believe you're insane
So pretend you're campaigning when you push that agenda
I'll mark you as unknown and return to sender

Prohibition Of A Word

Is that a snake in the grass or merely a viper
'nu komt de aap uit de mouw kruipen'[1]
It's amazing really what that sleeve conceals
If you roll it right up see what it reveals
A truth almost hidden behind another mask
If you didn't know 'de aantwoord'[2] I guess you'd have to ask
There are many different types of prohibition
Some of them subtle but still they cause division
Don't promote a bad meaning someone gave to a word
If you do in my view you will simply sound absurd
If denegrating words is really your mission
After hours of talking you just didn't listen
Its really incessant and frankly quite boring
I just fell asleep did you hear me snoring
Marijuana could never be deemed a racist word
That's all semantics or haven't you ever heard
To promote that as fact is a huge pile of shit
Deliberate division and it gets on my tits
I cannot be bothered to sit and explain
To those who don't listen again and again
Don't change it to say its prohibition derived
Thats twisting it round and just sounds contrived
When I read that crap it sounded bombastic
Empty fake words as natural as plastic
A hispanic word with it's origins a mystery
Though word prohibitionists try to rewrite history
So spreading that bullshit is a deliberate decision
For years now to stop it was a big part of my mission
But my mission is over I won't bother to talk
When it feels like I'm trying to educate pork

That kind of division is a prohibitionists tool
To promote it again you sound like a fool
Semantics is the philosophical meaning of words
I've said it so often maybe you never heard
Of course you didn't that's plain to observe
From now on I'll ignore you that's all you deserve
So please call me a drama queen see if I care
I'll worry about it whilst brushing my hair
Don't bother to call me I simply won't answer
I can't hear your tune and I'm just not a dancer
I did give it some thought that i must confess
Apologies if this has caused you distress
I believe what you do is deliberate action
And hope you achieved some strange satisfaction
To continue this path is not one that I choose
It is really unnecessary and will give me the blues
Our communal direction has come to the end
And has started to drive me clean round the bend
I'm choosing a new path but accept my best wishes
Cheerio and once again thanks for the fishes
I'm not doing this against you I'm doing it for me
Leave me alone and get back in the sea

[1] Now crawls the monkey out of the sleeve

[2] The answer

Infection Control

When trying to avoid unprecedented they really just trip on their words
When the depth of their thoughts merely sound bites integrity is seen as absurd

Keep on repeating infection control over and over again
Because you have blatantly lost the plot let me first explain

Give them some money via the council get it in a grant
But infection control, infection control two words to quickly implant

These are the reasons there is a war they tell us they are fighting
Of that there are no shortcomings except in the meaning of my writing

We're beating this virus and beating it together
Infection control though, what a marvellous endeavour

I laughed at their Care badges but some think them great
Remember they want you to think only they will put food on your plate

Infection control and this they do insist
Infection control you listen to this

Infection control now wash your hands
Drink up your coffee and wear rubber bands

Don't wear a facemask except where you must
Infection control it's the thing you can trust

A cleaner can clean now and a nanny can govern
Or is that from a witch? Oh no that's an oven

Infection control is the way we can manage
But that's not repairing it's more like a bandage

With infection control you control infections

So it cannot spread like unnatural selection

So infection control is my very best advice
Go on don't hang about you shouldn't think twice

And just in case you wondered or I forgot to mention
Infection control is really the best to control infection

Masking Something

Will you wear one in shops or on public transport?
To save other people if you cough, sneeze or snort

I've seen folks complaining so I just thought to ask
Of course I'm referring to the ubiquitous mask

The government announced we must wear them in shops
The enforcement of which at the discretion of cops

So why does this not fill my mind with confidence
Have you seen their behaviours with no fear of consequence?

Because legal and lawful don't really conjoin
Will they leave it to chance or the toss of a coin?

The government are only there to usurp us
Having proved once again they are not fit for purpose

Of course it's deliberate I mean the kerfuffle
Perhaps it's time for a cabinet reshuffle

Or even better a complete change of rules
Get rid of the toffs who treat us like fools

Although it is fake or an almost conundrum
Just say illegitimi non carborundum

It's all just some nonsense or even hyperbole
By the man at the top who has zero integrity

Every country in debt yes the whole of the planet
They won't stoke the fire and certainly won't fan it

So back to the start and the wearing of masks
What are they hiding everyone asks

But I don't mean the face things I mean politicians
When they made this announcement it aroused my suspicions
They are hiding something like their paedophile rings
But the show isn't over till the fat lady sings

Bleaching To The Subverted

I was gonna give this Dettol a try
And this please believe is no word of a lie
A local vicar tried it and now he is deceased
That's a thing I would call a bleach of the priest
I looked in the cleaning cupboard but all that I could find
Was an old carton of Vim stuck way, way behind
So at first I ignored it but then in the end

I snorted the stuff, now I'm clean round the bend
Later I remembered my disinfectant pine
Mixed it with some lemonade and it tasted really fine

Bender building

Army Boy with a well camouflaged String

FOOD FOR THOUGHT

Not only could cannabis be used as a medicine for our people but also as a medicine for our planet.

Fossil fuels are literally choking us all to death, whereas Hemp Biomass along with other sustainable energy forms are imperative, plastics made from plant materials rather than oil are a way towards a more sustainable future. Everything made from Hydrocarbons can also be made from Carbohydrates.

Textiles softer, more durable, fire retardant, mildew resistant, with inherent waterproofing qualities that can be grown without the use of Agrochemicals and pesticides that are depleting biodiversity.

Building materials that don't leach poisons into the earth either during manufacture and use that also act as a carbon sink.

Seeds more nutritious than Soya, easier to grow and even more importantly don't impede the body's take up of calcium essential for childhood growth.

Paper recyclable 7 times, unlike most other which can only be recycled 3 times.

The list continues with over 25,000 known uses for cannabis used for 1,000s of years in so many applications.

My Canna Journey;

I started as a recreational consumer of cannabis in 1974 during a lay over in Quebec Canada whilst serving in the Merchant Navy and continued through the years since. I was in a Road Traffic Accident in 1974 when my skull was fractured in two places along with many other superficial facial injuries. From then on I started having Migraines interspersed with Cluster Headaches the migraines were always severe and about 4 – 5 times a month, I managed these with cannabis use although I didn't realise this at till many years later when I learned of the Endocannabinoid system and how it functions to establish homeostasis.

> On March 24, 1992, Lumír Hanuš, a Czech analytical chemist working in Israel with American pharmacologist William Devane, isolated the first known endocannabinoid in the human brain. They named it anandamide, after the Sanskrit word for joy or bliss.

I have been active in my personal fight against prohibition for many years which originally only amounted to putting on Hemp Awareness displays and talking people through my research at non mainstream or alternative local fairs and festivals. I also attended many events such as the Cannabis Marches in London during the 1990s.

About 2003/4 I attended the annual conference of The Legalise Cannabis Alliance in Norwich. During this event I talked with many like minded souls and was persuaded to stand for parliament in 2005, a very strange thing for an anarchist to do. This made me step up my activism and put me in the view of the authorities, previously I had lived in the woods off grid so it was easy to hide, but from then on not so much.

Since those days I have had a plethora of health issues many of which are side effects of Chemotherapy and a Bone Marrow Transplant which I had after being diagnosed with Leukaemia in 2014. Although over the last two years I have been using Full Extract Cannabis Oil (FECO) to alleviate some of the symptoms these disorders are;

Fungal Pneumonia, COPD Emphysema, these have become more manageable with FECO

Epstein Barr Virus, This has now receded

Osteopenia. My bones are crumbling particularly in my spine the pain from which I cope with due to FECO

Also a little known disorder called Chemobrain, where my brain literally switches off I have found myself on more than one occasion standing in the middle of the road with no recollection of walking there, This also seems to no longer be an issue again I would presume due to my use of FECO

it also leads to odd allergies i.e. chocolate burns my mouth and sudden drops in energy, heart palpitations and difficulty in breathing when this happens I often just collapse in the street or wherever I am. The Anthony Nolan Trust have been conducting research into this disorder and finding more and more people have it, mostly from Breast Cancer and Leukaemia. I also suffer from nerve damage after chemotherapy which includes neuropathic spasms and areas of numbness the worst of which is my left arm which is completely numb right down to my fingertips and goes into uncontrollable spasms because my radial nerve was damaged during an operation to insert a 'PICC' line for the delivering of chemo and other medications, I find that FECO helps to alleviate most of the spasms and pain.

I have constant skin conditions where my skin just breaks out in scabs and is allergic to most soap and nearly every type of moisturiser I am often referred to the dermatologists at Kings Hospital for this, Cannabis balm helps this immensely.

I have had Osteoarthritis in both my knees and my shoulders for many years, which were helped by my use of cannabis. My left knee was due to be replaced in 2014 just at the time I was diagnosed with Leukaemia, this has been postponed indefinitely due to my condition but this leaves me walking with extreme pain, as there is no cartilage in my knees, I literally walk bone on bone. Although I have waited for years for a Total Knee Replacement because of my health they are unlikely to consider me for the operation, so once again...you've guessed it FECO it will be.

As I mentioned before I managed my headaches and pains from Osteoarthritis for many years using Cannabis, this worked well until I got leukaemia and needed a bone marrow transplant and because I had no immune system I was in an isolation room in hospital and had no access to Cannabis. After my transplant I contracted GVHD (Graft Versus Host Disease) this is fairly common with transplants as the immune system identifies the transplanted organ as a foreign object and attacks it, as this is common it is dealt with using immuno suppressant drugs. In the case of a Bone Marrow Transplant that is the immune system and can attack every organ which happened to me I was in so much pain I was screaming. I have a high pain threshold but that pain was unbearable the doctors put me on a constant Morphine drip, but also prescribed me with Tramadol and Codeine to help manage the pain, which did that job but left me unable to think properly, When I left the hospital and was home I soon got hold of some Cannabis and once again used it to alleviate the pain so I then stopped the morphine and I have found that when I can get hold of Cannabis I can function on a day to day basis. Of course Cannabis is illegal and therefore not always readily available so when I can't get it I live in a world of pain and cannot even make myself something to eat let alone go out of my home. Even with Cannabis my Osteoarthritis is painful and I use two walking sticks to get about, but without I am unable to stand without extreme pain and even moving around indoors often finds me crawling even to the bathroom.

I have also been diagnosed with Hyperthyroidism so my metabolism is all over the place, this also exacerbates the Osteopenia (insomuch as it effects my bone density) and COPD as it impedes my breathing and my heart races and hands shake for which they have offered me Beta Blockers which I've declined.

I know I am lucky to be alive for which I am very grateful and I could use the prescribed medications to alleviate my pains and disorders but I would have no quality of life under such a regime. Cannabis has given me some semblance of a life, I can socialise and engage in meaningful conversation which I found to be not possible on Opioids which I can have legally.

These days I try to educate people at every opportunity on the efficacy of Cannabis and FECO as an aid to homeostasis, and the nefarious reasons that Cannabis was demonised throughout the last century and as a former teacher imparting knowledge has always been one of my passions.

So as you can probably imagine my body is a painful place to be in on many occasions

And Yet I Smile

Medicinal, Recreational Or Whatever It's All Cannabis Use.

I think some people are missing some points about having a political party again.

In 2005 when I stood for the Legalise Cannabis Alliance in Canterbury I never once believed I was going to be an MP I did believe that this was the way to get the loudest message possible out. I had campaigned for medical cannabis at local festivals in Kent for some time and got a lot of interest not least of all from the Popo. I never felt I was doing anything wrong I am very aware that you have to be very careful how you phrase things i.e. we were giving out free cannabis seeds in the street with messages in them that did not encourage people to grow them but stated if they did grow them they could turn the plant into fuel, building blocks, jeans, etc. Had we said grow these and you can blah, blah, blah we would have been arrested for encouraging people to break the law. We also approached other parties and yes the greens are only fishing for votes, UKIP were an entirely different entity I didn't trust them at all i.e. do you know they would charge people foe visiting their GP check them out carefully. When I stood strange things started to happen in my life I had a permanent sick note that most people I knew weren't aware of my wife had just started her University course and my sickness benefit suddenly stopped as we had a new income (a student loan that we hadn't applied for) we had to apply for a student loan or I had to find a job great I had nearly died a couple of times that year but that's just background. We had moved out of the woods into a council flat which was then registered as my election address, the very next day a registered letter arrived informing me that we had to move a week later to a bigger flat as we were overcrowded, which I had told them many weeks before and was informed that we wouldn't be getting a move for at least 18 months.

We were on the top floor the intercom stopped working, my mail never arrived. I got beyond these things I'll tell you how if you are interested. I digress my point is I got 326 votes in the general election 325 more than I expected.

I was on BBCs Newsnight election special, that's high profile, some of the local police were interested in what I had to say they already knew me from my Big Issue days and talked about stuff, my wife convinced a sergeant to check out LEAP and later he told her that he and many of his colleague had joined.

I never got hassle from them only respect maybe now after a long break through illness things have changed but old bridges can be repaired that haven't been burnt. It's about having a loud voice for ending this sham of a democratic process over a plant that counts.

I never wanted the LCA to de register as a party I was one of the few that voted against at the Annual Conference in Norwich.

I believed then and now that we have a louder voice as a party than as a pressure group.

I don't believe that CLEAR have our interests at heart.

I believe that whatever an individual wants to use cannabis for is their right.

Some people think that only medicinal cannabis is a legitimate cause.

I have Leukaemia but I'm not primarily campaigning for medicinal reasons (unlike I did in the past, on someone else's behalf) but Recreation.

Look at the word RE Creation remaking yourself getting yourself together Recreating after a long day at work or whatever is just as legitimate as using cannabis for medicinal purposes.

WHEN DID PROHIBITION AS WE KNOW IT START?

There are many facets to why cannabis production, possession and distribution was and continues to be illegal. Anyone who has looked at this has heard of Anslinger, but may not of heard of Andrew Mellon he was the US Secretary of State for the Treasury from 1921 – 1932.

Anslinger a known racist (which in government circles was seen as acceptable back then) was married to his niece and was given the job as head of the federal bureau of narcotics; to vilify the name of hemp but using the word marijuana which nobody had heard of much.

The name marijuana is an old Mexican word that most western folks were unaware of but it does appear in Mexican Pharmacopeia from at least a hundred years before that time, most people however knew of cannabis as a medicine and hemp or low grade cannabis as is deemed more correct by many, for many other things including paper, fibres and ethanol its uses are endless so I'm not listing them here

Mellon was an investment banker and heavily invested in the upcoming fossil oil industries he was so rich he is said to have paid more taxes than anyone in the United States apart from John D Rockefeller or Henry Ford.

He was connected through investment to Lammot DuPont II who was the president of both DuPont and General Motors a company whose cars were built to run on fossil fuels whereas Fords still ran on alcohol which had also had a period of prohibition (1920-1933) because it was competition for the oil based industries and because they thought alcohol was bad for the health of the people.

It failed miserably (or did it) as people built stills but the period of illegality had allowed the petrol car industry to prosper. During the 13 years it lasted advances in engineering, manufacturing etc using oil were seen to make a lot of dosh. DuPont had just invented nylon and needed its competition knocked out. Nylon was an oil based copy of rayon which is made from plant matter often bark chips in the past before people covered their gardens with them.

The newspaper magnate Hearst had concerns that hemp could devalue his forests which were of course grown for newspapers amongst other things and he'd had a long history of vilifying both marijuana and Mexicans who he hated with a passion but that's another story and where the word marijuana was first pushed into the minds of westerners.

So it would seem that prohibition is an industry in and of itself

420

The origins of 420 have been questioned about for years some say this some say that however a reporter from interviewed a coupe of the original Waldos who were happy to talk as long as their names were left out of it.

Apparently in 1971 they had heard of a cannabis grow at Point Reyes Peninsula Coast Guard station, the grow belonged to a coast guard member that could no longer tend it, so armed with a treasure map they agreed to meet at 4.20pm by the statue of Louis Pasteur after athletics practice then they set off to find it. Although they searched for weeks and weeks they never found it, but did get very stoed trying and adopted the code 420 for going off to smoke.

There are many other stories but Chinese whispers seems to be rife amongst cannabis consumers

Locked Down In 420 Year

Another 420 another sunny day
But all the poor stoners were locked away
420, 420, the whole bloody month
If we go out will popo confront?
I'm just not a techy although I am speccy
I've never watched star trek so also not a trekkie
But lucky for us Danny Shine was there
Blazin in Hyde Park cos he just ain't scared
We were at home causing mayhem online
Saving it up for another good time

Blazing together with our virtual mates
Talking all over each other proper debates
People came and people went a really useful app
Ace giving really good advice me just talking crap
So thank you members of this cannafam for a really epic time
It gave us the chance to all catch up and for me another rhyme

Four Twenty

Four twenty four twenty they arrive in their plenty
But when we make a call just where are they all
They come in their thousands to smoke in the park
For civil disobedience and a bit of a lark
Some think this is how to protest this bad law
But it takes dedication and quite a bit more
But the thousands will come to smoke weed again
Of course far fewer if it's pouring with rain
If the weather is good though they'll be there en masse
The police just on standby ordered; do not harass
The police will ignore it till just after five
Then line up like shepherds with a stoned herd to drive
Just after five they'll arrest you again
If you're caught smoking cannabis I call that inane

You may think this is freedom but believe me it's not
When you go to four twenty to smoke all that pot
Now don't get me wrong I will also enjoy
But At the end of the day I'm still hoi polloi
I've said this before and it's never subliminal
In the eyes of the law I'll remain just a criminal
Some see the benefits some shut their eyes
Some still believe all the government's lies

The problem is really they have no integrity
They'll lie to each other and applaud their insincerity
But back to the park and everyone toking
The vapours rising from cannabis smoking
Ignoring a law that is obviously broken
With the knowledge this day is merely a token
So celebrate openly for just a few hours
The rest of the year you must hide all your flowers
So what is the point and why do I go?
To send out a message with knowledge to flow
These are things that everyone ought really to know
The way in which change will continue to grow
The seeds of the future must be planted anew
Have you guessed what I'm thinking does this give you a clue?
With a seed ripe for sowing there's only one way to go
Of course the clue is in the acronym GYO

Doom And Gloom

I don't wish to come across all doom and gloom
Though sometimes it feels I am stuck in this room
I'm not talking here of my physical reality
But the law here in Britain due to government mentality
I'll attempt to inform you and try to explain
Though my body is broken I still have my brain
Since the general election has something changed?
The government we have is still bent and deranged
I'm hoping to see as this new decade dawns an end to draconian laws
We could shout and shout till we're blue in the face and still only wear out our jaws
But I hope that I'm wrong as this new era starts
I can then stop campaigning and get down to some arts
When they said it was legal I knew it was bluff
It is fair to say I've just had enough
Of their lies in the media because nothing has changed

103

Remember though they are still bent and deranged
But much worse than that they have total autonomy
While between legal and lawful there remains little synonymy
Legal is merely a way to deceive
And make all the people simply believe
That legal is right but look to the past
The moral disparities are really quite vast
Legal isn't lawful that's unless you consent
To enforce cannabis laws means more tax money spent
The United Nations is quite likely to deschedule
So perhaps what they do will be quite influential
To weather this storm maybe needs an economist
With a view to the future so not an optometrist
But like government announcements I'm just playing with words
To show everybody how their thinking's absurd
There are so many arguments about schedule one
Prohibition needs banning and that's not just a pun

ABOUT THE AUTHOR

Rocky Van De Benderskum

Ex-tramp, Ex-teacher, writes poems and stuff
Ex-tremely inappropriate and if that ain't enough
One thing for sure he's too Punk to Funk
He don't drink booze so he never gets drunk
Leukaemia Survivor and his spirit is strong
He knows all the words can't remember the song
He loves to scribble and write stuff like this
He once stood for parliament if you want to reminisce
He lived in the woods for many a minute or two

Natural born anarchist if that gives you a clue
He fights for what's right and insists on the truth
He's a Geriactivist and he's long in the tooth

BOOKS BY THIS AUTHOR

What's In A Benderskum

Poems, anecdotes, scribbles in black and white and utter drivel

Inside My Hat And Other Heads

Poetry and stuff published by Alun Buffry including 13 poems by a benderskum

Words Of Weed And Wisdom

Poetry and stuff published by Alun Buffry including 25 poems by a benderskum

Printed in Poland
by Amazon Fulfillment
Poland Sp. z o.o., Wrocław

62169266R00068